Slammin' Simon's
Guide to Mastering Your First
Rock & Roll Drum Beats!

check out all the guides at
SlamminSimon.com

say hello at **slamminsimon@gmail.com**

© copyright 2015 Mark Powers
Simon and Rudi illustrations by Autumn Linde

Slammin' Simon plays . . .

REMO
drumheads

VIC FIRTH
drumsticks

and reads . . .

MODERNDRUMMER
magazine

Hello, hello – and welcome to
my *Guide to Mastering Your
First Rock & Roll Drum Beats!*

My name is Simon and playing drums is my
favorite thing in the world to do. I play so much,
my family and friends nicknamed me
Slammin' Simon.

My pet turtle is named Rudi,
short for the word "rudiment."

Rudiments are basic drum hand
patterns (or "stickings")
that are some of the most
important things for us
drummers to learn.

Rudi really likes to help me
(and *you!*) practice, by sharing
helpful reminders and tips.

We teach you all about rudiments in some of our other guides. In *this* one, we want to show you a whole bunch of basic Rock & Roll drumset grooves, so that you can get rockin' out in no time.

Are you all ready to get going?

Cool! Grab your drumsticks, take a seat behind your drumset and let's get started.

———————————————

Our drum music will be written like this...

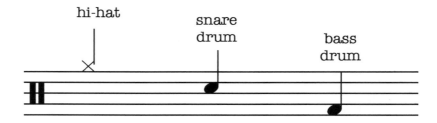

Before we jump into our Rock & Roll beats, we need to start off with a few exercises. First, let's play some simple notes called quarter notes. We'll play these on the hi-hat cymbals (sometimes just called the hi-hat).

This is the hi-hat here:

For now, whenever playing the hi-hat, keep the cymbals "closed" against each other by holding your left foot down on the hi-hat pedal.

When you play the quarter notes below,
count out loud, nice and steady. Don't speed up
and slow down when you count and play.

This is how we'll be counting:

"1...&...2...&...1...&...2...&..."

For now, only hit the hi-hat each time you say a
number (*"1"* or *"2"*) and *rest* (don't hit the hi-hat)
whenever you say the word *"&"*.

The "repeat sign" at the end of the measure of
music below means to repeat the pattern over
and over and over again. Keep going until you
are really comfortable with the rhythm.

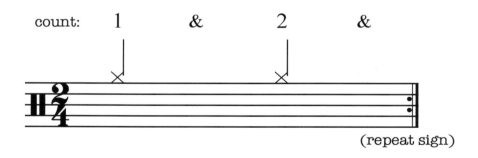

(repeat sign)

Next up, we also get to add in some bass drum!

The bass drum is the big, low sounding, drum
on the floor, that we play with a foot pedal.

Again playing quarter notes, put hi-hat and bass
drum together at exactly the same time.

Keep counting!

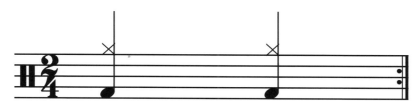

Here, instead of bass drum, play snare drum...

...along with the hi-hat.

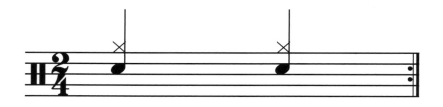

And now we finally get to combine all three of them
(hi-hat, bass drum and snare drum) at once!

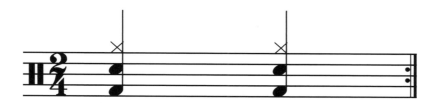

Put the hi-hat and bass drum together on beat 1...
and the hi-hat and snare drum together on beat 2
...and you're playing your first ever quarter-note
Rock & Roll drumset beat.

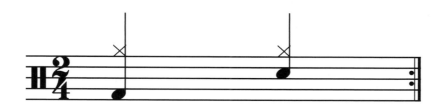

Got it? *Congratulations!*
Give yourself a pat on the back.

One more quarter-note pattern for you. This one is almost just like that last one, but with bass drum on both beats 1 and 2.

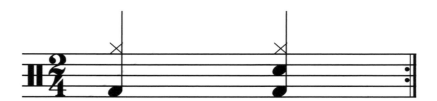

Sweet! Now we get to continue on and learn about one of my favorite kinds of notes: eighth notes!

Instead of resting when we count *"&"* each time, now the hi-hat will play on those, too.

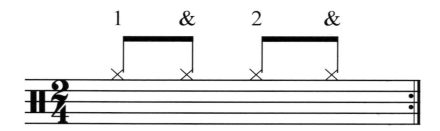

Hear how these eighth notes move along a little faster than our quarter notes? Pretty cool, I say :)

Time to add in some bass drum. Here are some great exercises that will get your hi-hat and bass drum working together really well.

Remember: don't stop counting.

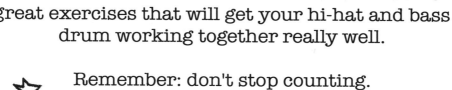

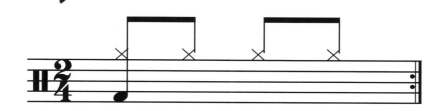

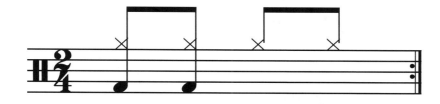

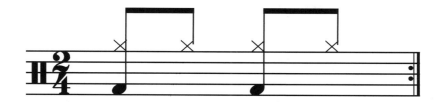

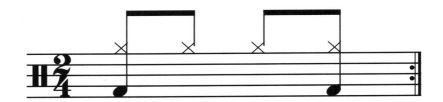

It's the snare drum's turn to play along with the hi-hat again. Here are a few more exercises, this time combining those two.

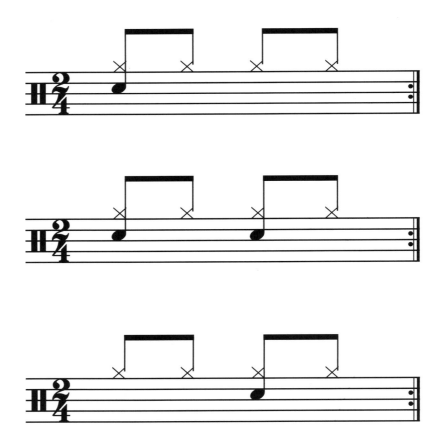

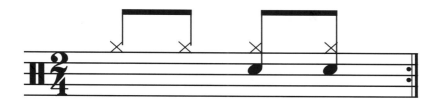

Now the real fun begins! While keeping the
hi-hat playing steady eighth notes, let's
experiment with all kinds of bass drum and snare
drum variations. These different combinations
give us a huge variety of eighth-note
Rock & Roll drumset beats to play.

Take your time as you work through these,
count out loud and keep your speed nice and even.
Don't try to go too fast right at first.

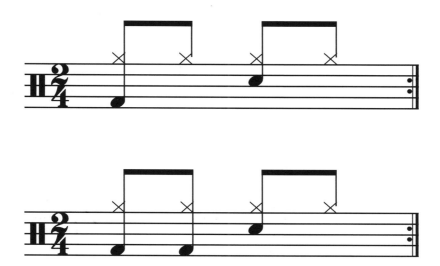

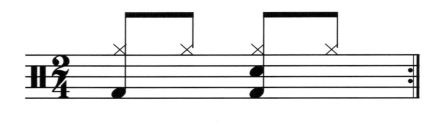

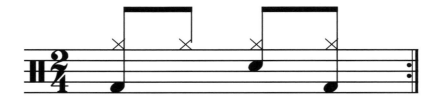

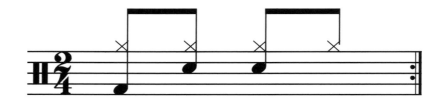

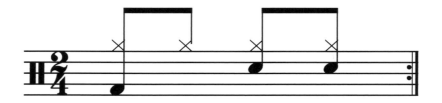

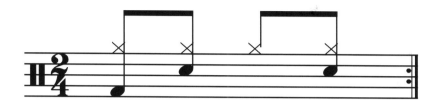

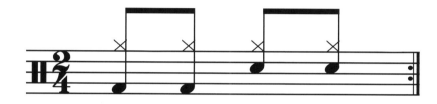

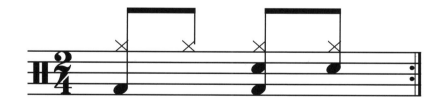

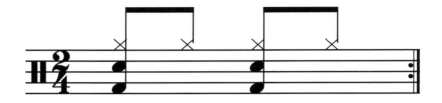

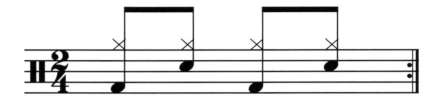

Got through all of those? High five! Wow, you
are seriously rockin'. What we get to do now
is make up some longer drum beats.

The ones we played before were two beats long,
and we counted them: *"1 & 2 &"*

Let's combine some of those earlier patterns
back-to-back and create some that are four beats
long, counted: *"1 & 2 & 3 & 4 &"*

Ready? Set. Go!

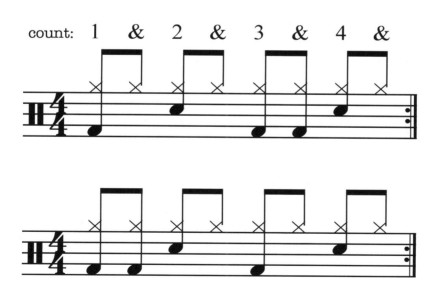

Rudi's Reminders

Three more *Turtle Tips*...

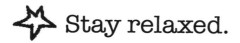 Stay relaxed.

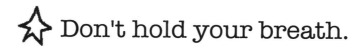 Don't hold your breath.

(this sounds silly but sometimes we do this when
we try playing faster or concentrate really hard)

⭐ Wear earplugs or headphones
when playing the drumset.

(to protect your hearing)

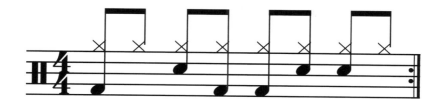

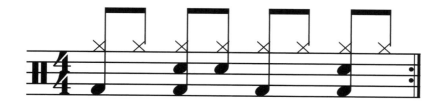

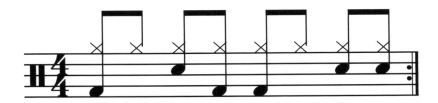

These are definitely not the only combinations that can be made from our short two-beat patterns. Mix-and-match all of them and you'll come up with even more awesome grooves!

Next up are some of my personal favorite drum beats. They use some of the ideas that the bass drum and snare drum have already played earlier in the guide, and some new ones. Hope you have fun with these...I always do.

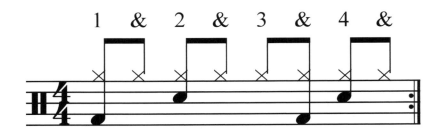

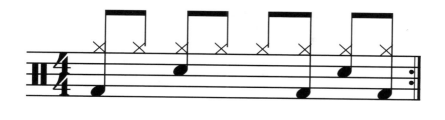

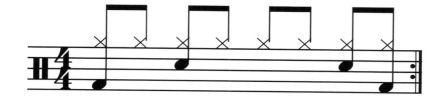

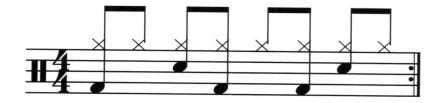

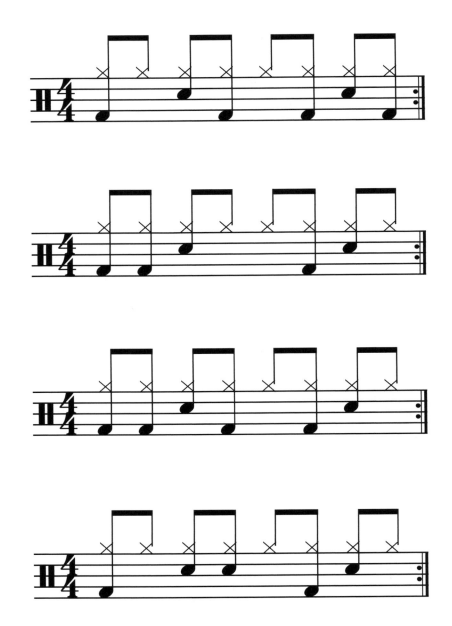

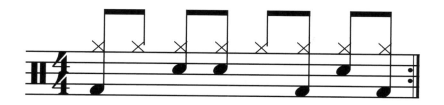

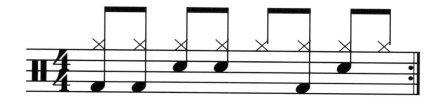

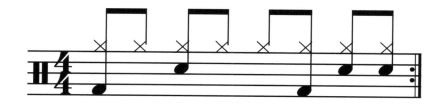

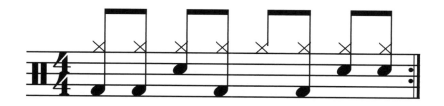

Nice job–you worked through the entire guide!
You should be well on your way to completely
mastering all of these beats.

Practice them a little bit every day, play along
with some of your favorite hit Rock & Roll songs,
and use your creativity to make up your own beats.
Keep at it and you'll improve week after week
until, someday, the drummer playing on the new
hit songs will be YOU!

Thanks for reading, and for letting me and Rudi
share all of these with you. When you get a
chance, message me at **slamminsimon@gmail.com**
and let me know what you thought about this guide.

Also, check out all my other guides at
SlamminSimon.com to learn even more
super awesome drum rudiments, grooves and fills.

You rock!

Slammin' X
Simon